NE   I0016326

America – Doomed and Damned

by Rock Hunter

TABLE OF CONTENTS

Forward

NEWTOWN, the present book, is built upon the over-riding theme of the prior Rock Hunter trilogy which is that good, honest questions and good, honest answers are necessary if TRUTH and VIRTUE are to advance human civilization. It is also the case, proven by the trilogy that such a Q-A approach to the monologues of dogma is shunned if not anathematized by the institutions of both church and state. The dogmatists of these institutions promulgate their own dictatorial agenda over monologues/lectures,/proclamations/declarations/fiats/ and all related egocentrisms which means that for these egocentrisms to remain intact and rewarded with praise and money, they must also suppress good, honest Q-A sets. The emperor can continue with his naked delusion only as long as nobody asks a forthright, good, honest question about his clothes. Vanity of vanities, all is vanity we read in the book of Ecclesiastes.

What is a book? If we say that a book is a collection of words, we may then ask what is meant by "word"? At the beginning of the Gospel of John we read, "In the beginning was the word and the word was with God and the word was God". Something has been placed on a page to denote the source of everything which exists, that all-powerful source, which must therefore be "ineffable", inscrutable or abstract to a degree which we cannot even imagine. We are then told that this Word became a flesh and blood man, Jesus. The abstract or metaphysical became concrete or physical and He declared that His words (plural) would never pass away (Matthew 24:35).

Catholic Catechism Critique (CCC) by Rock Hunter put into practice the Catholic Catechism paragraph 801 directive to "test all things" but there is no difference between a test which proves a religious event and a test to prove any other event. CCC closed with two broad truth tests referred to as NEWTOWN and Newtown.. NEWTOWN capitalized has to do with an idealized civilization for 100,000 Americans. What would a city or habitat of 100,000 be like if the population were living a Catholic lifestyle for example? Or, how would they live with Donald Trump as their president? His current (2016) campaigning stands on a Christian platform – or so he says. Yet, who can tell him how to build and operate such a civilization? Where are the experts? Are they in the Vatican or Magisterium of Roman Catholicism? Are they at Liberty University or Southern Baptist Theological Seminary ?

Newtown has to do with **truth testing** of a forensic theory which pertains to the terrifying events in Newtown, Connecticut on Dec 14 and Dec 16 of 2012 when the world was apprised of the mass murder of 20 children plus six adult staff at Sandy Hook Elementary School (SHES) plus shooter and his mother (14/12). Later, on 16/12, another terrorist similarly threatened St Rose of Lima, school and church complex. Since he has not been arrested, the community still lives in fear of a terrorist gang at large; a gang which could strike again at any time."NEWTOWN", the present book, begins where CCC left off.

The NEWTOWN test will hereafter be Canadianized and generalized/universalized as CANOPOLIS. **Canada, not America, is now the ideological leader of the Free World**..What would any civilization of 100,000 be like, fitted into the great mosaic of the Canadian Confederation, perhaps as a reservation nested within a Sovereign First Nation (which might also be a member of the UN General Assembly)? Moreover, the natural language monologues and question-answer dialogues which set out the structure and functioning of a CANOPOLIS or the forensic theories concerning 14/12 can be described in a computer program. C language is suggested, with Stephen Prata's text as reference manual. But Q-A is a language as well.

SHAI-SHAL

What would we call a robot which dispenses comprehensive knowledge in a natural language program (NLP)? If it literally aspires to ALL knowledge (as academia does), why not call it GODBOT? GODBOT would then be the teacher of NEWTOWN and Newtown testing and potentially all else pertaining to civilization and its progress. Having read the present book, the reader should understand beyond any doubt that the Turing Test, correctly articulated, could have been passed long ago and that GODBOTS which can teach better than humans by various measures in many classroom situations have also been available for a long time. A new era has begun with robots like Nao and BB-8 entering homes, offices and classrooms. Though online and partially automated education has been available for some time, it has had limited acceptance because of the human equivalency problem. As students we require a teacher approximating a human personality. That is what humanoid robots provide. The exorbitant cost of present day higher education will be seen as a malady associated with this stage in our civilization comparable to the malady of streets filled with sewage and garbage before these problems were solved by modern engineering.

Why only program robots as AI and AL (Artificial Life) forms to catch up to humans? Why not think in terms of SHAI (Super-Human AI) and SHAL (Super-Human AL)? What happens when we have robots in society with intelligence superior to humans and vital signs superior to humans? Present technology can already build these robots. For example, a Hawkingbot model at Cambridge could teach mathematics and physics better than Stephen Hawking, play chess better, spell and define words better and it would display measures of vitality to surpass those of Hawking. Apply CC p 801 "test all things" scientific measures: Can it not tell better jokes in the classroom? Can it not walk and chew gum better? What would a GODBOT say in the "God Quad" at Notre Dame University, streaming "God Tube" information from Xulon Press? In other words it would function as an ebook with audio-video and voice in/voice out abilities. Could it teach CC better than Pope and Magisterium? Could it teach CCC better than Rock Hunter?

.

Those "test all things" measures tell us that in Connecticut today there is a blackout of important information relevant to the events of 14/12/12. Confirmation of the Newtown tests begun in CCC continues with the book NEWTOWN. Americans have traditionally color-coded their states with Democrat-associated red and Republican-associated blue. Now we need a new color which is black, for those states where the five foundational freedoms with associated rights of the US Constitution have been blacked out or ablated. Connecticut is the first black state. Donald Trump and Governor Jesse Ventura (who wants to be his Vice President) do not give political speeches in Connecticut today, expectedly for fear of assassination. One has to wonder about the credibility of White House wannabes like these two. They cannot even defend their own constitutional and human rights and freedoms. Now they want to be recognized by all the people of America and the Free World as their leaders.

.To confirm this information blackout in Connecticut, apply "test all things" to some good, honest questions about 14/12/12 through the offices which administer Freedom of Information laws (<foi@ct.gov> and Child Advocacy laws <oca@ct.gov>. For example, how many children attended schools other than SHES before 14/12/12 and how many after (since the 500 children said to have survived the terror were reportedly taken in by those schools)? When someone as brave as former Navy Seal Ventura cowers under his bed in fear, you know the beginning of a widespread regime of terror in America has begun. Neither he nor Trump dares to exercise the right/freedom of religion and go to St Rose of Lima Church/School in Newtown where Governor Malloy addressed the audience on 16/12/12 after which another terrorist phoned in to say (repeatedly) he would finish the job which alleged shooter Adam Lanza had started on 14/12. Of course a SWAT team quickly arrived but the terrorist (and perhaps terror gang) is still at large.

THE FINAL AMENDMENT

It is not the freedom and right of bird watchers to assemble, petition, speak and so on, about birds which has been paid for in blood and treasure to create what we call the Free World. It is the freedom and right to do so on **controversial matters, often in the political-religious domain.** Trump-Ventura cannot express freedom of religion at Rose of Lima (ROL) or any other public place in Connecticut. That means their right/freedom of assembly is denied. They cannot express the issues in writing so rights/freedoms of the press (journalism) are denied as are rights/freedoms to petition judicial and governing authorities and press important concerns. Note the use of the word "press" as verb as well as noun. It is an action word. Of course freedom of speech on important matters is denied. The unpopular 18th Amendment (Prohibition) was ablated (revoked) by adding a 21st amendment with this effect. Today there is an unspoken **Final Amendment** which has guided the US President (Obama) and Cabinet (Clinton et al) in Newtown and Connecticut. The Final Amendment ablates the foundational rights and freedoms for the rest of the US Constitution which means the constitutions throughout the Free World. And the aspirations for the rest of civilization which yearns to be free. **CONNECTICUT IS NO LONGER PART OF THE FREE WORLD**.

Canadian journalism tycoon, (His Excellency) Lord Conrad Black says he is an old friend of Trump's. Let him prove this political theory wrong. Why not start a new Black newspaper in Newtown and region to compete with the current Bee and Courier? Why not put forward the following outlandish theory about what really happened on 14/12/12 in this Black newspaper to liberate a black state? This theory comes from a pdf file sent by Professor James Fetzer which will be referred to as the Fetzer Report. The complete citation is in the References section. It is in opposition to the position of officialdom which is called the Sedensky Report.

THE FETZER REPORT

In 2009, Obama-Clinton et al sent a paramilitary squad of 20 or so terrorists into Newtown. All, if not most, were given free. ½ million dollar houses (a number of them on Christmas Day). These acquisitions are verifiable from property titles offices. They were part of what military science calls a Gladio operation which means they are trained soldiers who are allowed to use deadly force as required but usually they operate in plain clothing like undercover police.

SHES had been vacant since 2008 and remained so until 2012 when it was used to stage what was communicated to the world as a terrifying massacre. Observations by Fetzer at al say that about a half dozen features of SHES prove it was a derelict building such as asbestos contamination, roofing leaks, loose wires and mold on the walls. In addition, there was no handicap parking place marked at the school in 2012 as required by federal and state laws. United Way moving company brought in the stage props for the bogus massacre of 20+6 (children + staff) who were attending the school out of about 500+70 total.. Miraculously United Way had set up a charity fund for the survivors several days earlier. During the morning of the staged massacre, journalists were kept at a distance but what the few still and moving pictures available do show is a small crowd (of paid actors) strangely milling about the SHES entrance. There were no ambulances in attendance. Another miracle had happened. This was the miracle of medical diagnosis when a brilliant and unidentified medical expert determined immediately that all 26 + shooter were dead and did not need hospital diagnosis. Later there was the Hochsprung miracle when Hochsprung (a staffer who was among the dead) resurrected for a media interview. There is also the miracle of the disappearing 500+70 because no school has reported taking them in. There are other anomalies in the official story, the Sedensky Report, anomalies so extreme that the word miracle applies well.

Thus you can see why a Trump-Ventura political-religious speech at Rose of Lima is apropos and you have a better understanding of the Rock Hunter letter from the Courier newspaper of Newtown-Monroe which was printed in CCC.

TEST ALL THINGS

All of this might be comical as a badly flubbed and absurd drill by FEMA, a drill which was expected to also promote the gun control cause in America. The Catholic Catechism p 801 "test all things" rule could settle it for all concerned fast if FOI and OCA offices would give the statistics requested.. Also, what were the expenditures on janitorial supplies from 2008-2012 at SHES as well as any measures of electrical, water and fuel usage? The comedy ends when we consider that Adam Lanza and his mother Nancy Lanza do not appear to be part of the White House sourced terror gang of 20 dating from 2009. They were long standing members of the community and the evidence to date is that both were murdered under the White house orders of Obama-Clinton et al (meaning the entire Cabinet is culpable). Where are the "heroic Catholics" called for by Bishop Jenky from Peioria, Illinois?. That expression in quotes is his. With a congregation of 250,000 one might expect a few to go to the trouble given the awesome implications of 14/12. It is also deemed sinful for a Catholic to not obey any one of the 2,865 paragraphs in CC. Is p 801 now an exception?.

THE BRAVE AND THE NOBLE

Trump and Ventura could settle the matter by applying that "test all things" rule and exercising their constitutional rights and freedoms. Alas those rights and freedoms have been ablated by the Final Amendment. It would be tempting to say then that until Trump and Ventura go into Connecticut and liberate that State, they are cowards who are not fit to lead America and certainly not fit to lead the free World. Does the liberation of Connecticut await a Black Ribbon Day newspaper from Lord Black? Black Ribbon Day was the name given to a Toronto-based movement during the Cold War with a purpose of helping to free nations under Soviet-Marxist tyranny. In the unlikely event that the Fetzer Report is wrong about a Gladio military squad from the White House having been located in Newtown in 2009, then the Trump-Ventura team can do the noble thing and defend the honour of Obama-Clinton and Cabinet. "All" it requires is access by **FREEDOM of information laws which can be used this way in all remaining FREE States of America and of course, Canada**. How many children (and staff) WERE there in other Newtown schools just before and just after 14/12/12? Those two numbers alone are enough to debunk the Fetzer Report. In addition there are audits on janitorial supply expenditures from 2008-2012 and related physical numbers to show water, electricity and fuel usage. The same data could prove any house suspected of being a crime scene to have been in operation or not in use. **To exonerate Obama-Clinton of all suspicion for this heinous criminality is so simple and inexpensive**. Those noble men Trump and Ventura can surely come to the rescue of Clinton as damsel in distress. Otherwise does it take the intervention of the British Nobleman, His Majesty Lord Conrad Black using a Black newspaper to liberate a "black" State?

Preface

"NEWTOWN" is intended to be a model of precis writing. Every effort has been made to say as much as possible in as few words as possible. It is built upon the knowledge base of the "Rock Hunter Trilogy", three previous books titled The Jew Who Said He Was God (TJWSHWG), Gold War, and Catholic Catechism Critique (CCC). The first two were published by Xulon and the third by Friesen. How can these be summed up in precis style?

THE JEW WHO SAID HE WAS GOD

TJWHSWG presents the issue of "What the Bible really tells us" as a matter of binary choices (which are like the choices made by man, mouse and machine in maze running). If we are free at the choice points of decision-making, then what are those key choice points in life? In the beginning _____ In the beginning, what? What do Genesis and the Gospel of John say? "In the beginning, God. There is no verb in that sentence., no past, present or future tense. One can make a choice at our present choice point and believe, "In the beginning, Big Bang". But most academic cosmologists, including Hawking say there is a multiverse and not just a universe. Why should every universe start with a big bang? When this universe ends, will it restart with a big bang or some other beginning? The choices go on. But physicists like Hawking do not understand metaphysics. "Big Bang" is a "singularity" which means the rules of physics do not apply to the Big Bang per se. They apply only after the Big Bang.. To talk about a beginning of time is an oxymoron because it requires the concept of time at a stage when time has not yet happened. God transcends time and space. Where were you when I created the universe, He asks Job and his friends.

The Story of TJWSHWG is irrefutably a historical event from 2,000 years ago which even the Atheist will not deny as far as the existence of the Story is concerned. The disputes (choices) have to do with its various issues but the main one is about the IDENTITY of the heroic or central figure. Even if the Story is metaphorical or fable, is this plausibly the nature of the Almighty? If the Story is not a reference to a real life Jesus Christ (unlikely though that is), is it sound theological theory? This results in an overall choice (the validity of TJWSHWG) and many particular choices. Those particulars could lead to the articulation of a computer program in C for GODBOT which would answer all the questions of CANOPOLIS. Will GODBOT be programmed with truth or lies to guide "Future Sapiens" as Earth civilization expands throughout all future time and space? Do we want to live by truth or by lies, here and throughout this small universe with its billions of stars x billions of galaxies over billions of years? Since TJWSHWG said I came to tell the truth and I am the way, the truth and the life, GODBOT should be programmed accordingly.

Institutions of both church and state claim to have TRUTH as their ideal and objective. As the opening words of this book say, however, the Q-A sets necessary for the hierarchy of truths to shine through the darkness of ignorance requires a change in the norms of these institutions. There is no recorded instance of TJWSHWG rejecting a good, honest question. GODBOT, honestly programmed by honest people would apply this standard to monologue/lecture units as well as subsequent Q-A sets. The imaginary scenario is worth repeating. Imagine GODBOT (perhaps a model which looks like Stephen Hawking) teaching from the God Quad at Notre Dame using the GodTube audio-visual aids of Xulon press. This is not "New Age" heresy unless those programming the teaching machine make it so. What if Oxford were to hire Hawkingbot as a competitor to Hawking at Cambridge?

GOLD WAR

Gold War announces the discovery of a trillion dollar gold field in British Columbia in the context of the OE (Old Earth) and YE (Young Earth) theories pertaining to Intelligent Design and Creation Science. No other gold field on Earth is in this league other than Wits Basin in South Africa so this could make BC the most mineral wealthy nation in the world or at least number two and trying harder. BC will balkanize soon, however, as First Nations take seats in the UN General Assembly so it may be renamed (like Ceylon, Persia and Siam; Peking and Bombay) Gold War uses YE models to discover the gold field, arguing that the OE models of gradual/Darwinian evolution and historical geology are grossly inadequate. (1) Where have the huge deposits of sediments gone? They are predicted by OE to be higher than several Everests. (2) What makes the "rock clocks" of OE valid? Where is the proof that radioactivity stops in magmas and starts in cooled-solid rocks? (3) Why are the continents mostly granitic (felsic) rock since they are being constantly replenished by basaltic (mafic) rock from the mantle below? The great flood basalts on the continents and the ocean floor below recent sediments are mafic rock of mantle origin. (4) Where is there proof in the rocky fossil record that even one new species could develop hard tissue like bone from mutation when countless attempts to do so in laboratories have failed? (5) Where is the evidence of human civilization during the last mild interglacial period dating to about 100,000 years ago? This mild interglacial should have produced a burgeoning of civilization with abundant ruins and artifacts as we see now during the present interglacial warm period.

Past geological chronologies as preached in generally accepted academic dogma (GAAD) are woefully inadequate. It is possible that an "act of nature" can also be "an act of God" The two ideas are not mutually exclusive. The miracles which God generated for Moses and the Israelites (for example the plagues and the parting of the Red Sea) may have had natural counterparts like interplanetary events, plate shifts and volcanoes as well as supernatural sources which is to say, from God. There are a number of events like this from the Bible like the fall of Jericho which secularists try to explain only naturally. What was the blast from heaven which destroyed the army of Sennacherib? It could have been a bolus fall from volcanic or interplanetary origin as well as an act of God. The Netflix documentary series, "Secrets of the Bible" shows both secular and religious experts at work trying to shed more light on the dramatic events described in the Bible. Drill cores from the Black Sea floor for example prove major stratigraphic disruptions. One of these may have coincided with the Great Flood and the source of the water could have been extra-terrestrial. Fine ice crystals from space could have fallen on this planet and turned to rain. Some day this planet may pass through a dust cloud in space.

In future chronology, Future Sapiens is expected to learn genetic engineering and transgenics so as to be able to populate new planets accreted from space rubble by Future Sapiens with new species Indeed, conventional geological theory posits that this planet was formed out of an interplanetary collision after which rocky plates accreted. Could they not have accreted while carrying fossils from alien worlds? The dinosaurs may still be alive … on another planet. "When we've been here 10 million years, bright shining as the sun". Does Present Sapiens (Homo Sapiens) think no species with SHAI-SHAL capabilities among those billions of stars x billions of galaxies (or beyond them) could possibly have achieved this in the past? Since tardigrades can live in the cold of space for weeks and ejecta from volcanoes and bolide collisions send these and other creatures off-planet on rocky space ships, why would panspermia not be the rule of the cosmos? Never talk to aliens, Stephen Hawking's momma told him. They might be just interplanetary space bugs which regard Homo Sapiens as tasty snack food. They might also be immensely more brilliant than you.

If we could see the technologies of Future Sapiens today, many would be rated by us as miraculous. Sto:lo Indians who are the original inhabitants of Vancouver and region say their early history was generated by "Sky-born people". Are these the people of Genesis 1 compared to the "Earth-born people" of Genesis 2? Sky-born people are associated with an era of miracles when animals could speak to people (like the snake in Eden or Balaam's ass?) and amazing transformations of culture took place. Maps even show the places in this region where Sky-born people descended from the heavens.

Define the word, miracle.

CATHOLIC CATECHISM CRITIQUE

CCC has done what no other book has done previously over the many centuries of the Catholic Church. It has examined the **2,865 paragraphs of Pope-and-Magisterium-claimed-truths** in CC and found them to be profoundly inadequate, with many untruths, great and small. This comprehensive compendium of doctrine did not exist as a single volume until the era of Pope John Paul II (Mr Wojtyla). Here is an example of the CCC reasoning. If St Mary is, as claimed, mother of all the living, she must be mother of herself. If she can be presented with all prayers which she deals with as effectively as TJWSHWG (as CC claims) then she can be presented with the Lord's Prayer (the only formal prayer given to us by TJWSHWG). But the Lord's Prayer is comprehensive which requires all power for actualization. Only God has all power. Therefore CC says St Mary is God. CC also says Allah is God because it claims that Muslims worship the same God as Catholics even though Koran repudiates the Holy Trinity of Catholicism, saying such believers will be punished harshly. CC has then put forward two other "Gods" alongside the Triune God. It has proclaimed a Holy Quintet.

NEWTOWN will proceed with precis writing like this. As the CANOPOLIS program is written, why waste words in C source code, binary object code or the Standard Everyday English (SEE) translation? The CANOPOLIS program will be an exercise in NLP (Natural Language Programming).

Imagine then a contest of civilizations across Canada, each with a population of 100,000 and each nested within a sovereign First Nation as a "reservation". We currently see such mass immigration as thousands of Syrians enter Canada. How would 100,000 NEWTOWN people live as America's "best of the best" to use a Donald Trump slogan? Located on and around one of BC's many mountains, what would make this the shiniest city on a hill, brighter and better than every other CANOPOLIS? The ultimate ideal is what we call perfection. Isn't that what we strive for, even while we realize that on our own we cannot attain it? Do we go to a restaurant and ask for an imperfect meal or the closest to a perfect meal which can be provided? Do we ask a dentist to imperfectly fill that tooth or do we ask for his best work, that which is closest to perfection? The perfect power over all things then becomes synonymous with all power. GODBOT, CANOPOLIS and NEWTOWN are all about imperfect approximations to God's perfection. Newtown is about the perfecting of a forensic theory with awesome national and international implications.

EARTH II

The debate between young and old Earth opinions has gone on for generations. Much of this is speculation because common sense tells us the further back in time we go, the more difficult it is to be certain about what really happened. However, it would help to imagine Earth II as a younger planet than the one we have now with a mantle of dark and dense mafic rock, some of which is molten and gets squeezed up to the surface. The vertical paths would use fractures and faults in the rock as well as pipes so the surface formations would range from huge sheets as we see now on the spreading ocean floor (oceanic crust), smaller floods of lava as we see presently with flood basalts and also localized volcanic mounds and elongated formations from small local faults.

Water would cover most of this mafic planet and perhaps all of it at times. But islands would appear and some of the islands would be large and could be called continents like Australia. Once rocks of any kind are exposed to the surface, they are subject to the forces of erosion. Atmospheric erosion in the past may have been more violent or less violent than today. If it was comparable to today's erosion, then as Gold War explains, the old Earth thinking of conventional geology is very questionable, at least as far as old continental crust is concerned. That brings in the reasonable consideration of "Thorist" forces to use a neologism in Gold War. In addition to the "Plutonist" and "Neptunist" forces recognized by conventional geology, we must consider the forces of other planets, planetoids, asteroids, moons, meteors, meteorites, comets and clouds of dust and chemicals in space. All of these along with radiation and magnetic fields from space can impact here, again and again through our astrogeological history. The impacts may be natural and random. They may also be due to intelligent design and creative/creation science which means super-natural.

The idea of an interplanetary collision followed by accretion of large chunks of rock to create the Earth and Moon is now in vogue with academic dogmatists (GAAD). Why could large chunks or plates of rock not arrive here again and again after that? Might they not carry fossils and even live species, especially if they are accreted by intelligent emplacement? Of course not, say the dogmatists … WE will some day do this kind of work as WE create new planets and populate them but nobody "out there" in space could do this and of course WE know by fiat that panspermia could not be the norm of the cosmos and WE know that species generated from panspermia "out there" could not be more intelligent than us. Vanity of vanities, all is vanity. That is GAAD.

Prelude

Newtown, the SHES story, is a prelude to the general programming of humanoid robots now entering the homes, offices and schools of society. That programming is their (artificial) acculturation. It is an acculturation which all members of society must undergo. Infants are acculturated. Mental patients are "normalized" and that too is acculturation. Even pets are acculturated; otherwise they are called pests Humanoid robots now entering society go by names like Nao (pronounced "now") and BB-8. Nao has a population of over 5,000 in over 50 nations. It is as appropriate to give population estimates for this new species undergoing creation and evolutionary development as it is for extant species like humans or elephants.

MORAVEC TESTS

The Turing Test was passed long ago. Is the speaker on the other side of the wall a human or machine? That is the Turing test question. Imagine then a humanoid robot which uses a face mask and body outline in the image and likeness of Stephen Hawking perhaps drawing on the London Wax Museum work and it has the same voice synthesizer. Program this GODBOT, Hawkingbot model, to do classroom teaching at Cambridge or perhaps have a Cambridge-Oxford competition between man and machine. Would Oxford hire Hawkingbot? It delivers lecture-monologues and handles student questions afterward (these are Question-Answer, or Q-A sets). It would have to be "dumbed down" to pass the Turing Test. It would teach mathematics and physics so much better than Hawking that the person rating performance would know it was a Robo Sapiens and not the Homo Sapiens, Hawking. Hawkingbot will also pass Turing tests if it is programmed to babble like a human at around 1 ½ years of age or programmed to simulate the speech of many mental patients whose verbiage is quite arcane. A broader and better expression is Moravec Test rather than Turing Test. Roboticist, Hans Moravec calls for "human equivalency" testing. It also applies to AL (Artificial Life) testing. For example, is the lecturer on that distant stage in dim light the real Hawking or Hawkingbot?

The moral to this story is also that if the game of natural language programming (NLP) is rigged, good, honest questions will not be countered with good, honest answers and the robot will be made to sound much more stupid than it is. Technolords have worked zealously and for many years to suppress humanoid robots and good, honest testing of human equivalency. That "dumbing down" is what CCC also proves to have been done by the so-called teaching masters who wrote CC. "Iron Side" was the name of a television series about a wheelchair-bound lawyer. What would Hawkingbot teach in a law classroom about the Newtown/SHES Story?

The GODBOT software of our intrepid courtroom lawyer would lecture on the current lawsuit by 10 claimants who say they were victims of the 14/12/12 shooting by Adam Lanza. These claimants want the case heard by a jury as well as a judge, expecting that a jury will be biased toward the bogus victims who were as a whole members of a criminal gang located in Newtown in 2009 and given free houses (easily proved or disproved) at that time. Program GODBOT then to address the jury for the defense. Defendants are Bushmaster, the maker of the gun supposedly used by Adam Lanza <info@bushmaster.com>, Camfour the firearms distributor and Riverview Gun Sales retailer which sold the gun to Nancy Lanza in 2010 and closed soon after 14/12.

Ladies and gentlemen of the jury. For every civil suit there is a countersuit. First I will defend my clients with some statements and then I will summarize the basis for countersuit. This suit says my clients have done nothing to warrant penalization because there was no functional SHES between 2008 and 2012. Since the school was a derelict building in disrepair and not functional there could not have been any terrifying event impacting approximately 500 students and 70 staff on 14/12 as the complaints say. There was no mass shooting, no mass murder. There does however appear to be selective shooting and killing but none of this faults my clients.

The proof of the non-functionality for SHES can be obtained under freedom of information laws <foi@ct.gov> and child protection laws <oca@ct.gov>. **If 500 children were forced to occupy SHES on the morning of 14/12, 2012, with its asbestos contamination, leaking roof, loose wires, mold and absence of marked handicap parking, that was severe child abuse**. That would be one possible countersuit … but there was no functioning school. FOI reports on janitorial supply expenditures between 2008 and 2012 will prove that as will records of electrical, water and fuel usage, some of which is metered. Total school attendance at schools other than SHES just before and just after 14/12 will prove that the 500+70 were not in attendance at SHES before 14/12 because they were not relocated after 14/12 to other schools. FOI and OCA offices deny this information so I will request a court order to have it released.

The main theme of the **countersuit in preparation** is that a terrifying event was undeniably communicated to the entire community of Newtown and surroundings. Mental illness is communicable illness as the medical research proves. Even well trained professionals suffer anxieties, depressions and a host of other illnesses, contracted by communication from their patients. Many thousands of people suffered post-traumatic effects as our survey of the community (in preparation) will establish.. The complainants in this countersuit may number, not 10 but tens of thousands. The defendants will be those who staged the shooting on 14/12, mainly using a Bushmaster .223 caliber rifle and those who selectively murdered the long-standing citizens of Newtown, Nancy and Adam Lanza.

Chapter 1: Innocent Bot In A Not-So-Innocent World

GODBOT enters this world, perhaps uttering the text of BCIT's first lesson in C programming:

HELLO WORLD!

GODBOT is as innocent as a new-born baby. What it says and does is exactly according to programming. If it lies, that is only because it is programmed to lie. It has no choice or intent in the matter. If it were programmed to tell the truth, the whole truth and nothing but then truth as a Lawbot, what would it say about 14/12/12 in defense of Bushmaster et al?

First there is a question of whether any court in Connecticut at this time remains uncorrupted. Therefore **Connecticut judges are expected to deny them the right to defend themselves by presenting the most important evidence necessary** which is proof that the school was not in use between 2008 and 2012 and in confirmation, there was no sudden influx of 500+70 into nearby schools after 14/12. Remember the previous assertion that the mission of Obama-Clinton et al (White House Cabinet) was to take Connecticut out of the Free World. All important rights and freedoms are ablated by the Final Amendment which now rules in tyranny over the people of Connecticut. Otherwise, GODBOT would simply enter the court and say, Your Honor, my clients are not culpable in the SHES 14/12 mass murder by .223 Bushnel because there was no functional SHES. There was no attendance by 500 students and 70 staff so these people could not have been victims. After that the judge will say, Then you have the proof of this? GODBOT will reply that it has requested the proof under Freedom of Information laws and State authorities (like FOI and OCA offices) are required by law to provide the requested information. The judge who has sold his soul to tyranny will laugh up his black robed sleeve and adjourn. On next meeting the innocent GOBGOT will address this guilty and corrupt judge and say the information has been illegally denied by State authorities and thus a court order is requested to obtain the information. This court order could also be requested even before the civil proceedings begin in court. However, **since justice and its associated rule of law have been ablated in Connecticut by the Final Amendment, no judge will issue a court order to have the information released by OCA and FOI.**

GRAND JURY

Given that the judicial process is rigged under White House tyranny and a puppet Governor, given that the so-called opposition (people like Trump and Ventura and millions of "heroic Catholics") now cower in fear, what alternative is there other than the hideous prospect of bloody civil war? There is the grand jury of the general public, all those who are potential jurors in any courtroom proceeding. We tend to take the RIGHT to trial by peers for granted. It was won at great cost since historically our ancestors did not have this right and today most of the world still does not have this right. The complainants in the Bushmaster et al case say they want trial by jury. Let them have it, in spades. Go to the jury of the general public. Why waste time and money in a criminal Connecticut court?

It is irrefutable that an entire community was terrified by REPORTING/COMMUNICATING of the SHES events on 14/12 and the terrifying threat at St Rose of Lima (a church and school complex) when a telephone caller said repeatedly that he would finish the work Adam Lanza had started. The building and surroundings were vacated for a SWAT team. This terrorist caller (in layman's usage of that word, terrorist) is still at large. Some people must reasonably think that 14/12 may have involved more than one person ... perhaps a terrorist gang which is still a threat. This adds to the value of resolving the matter fully, once and for all. Therefore a start is the submission of a questionnaire on post-14/12 psychological effects. The following is a rough draft of that questionnaire which can be finely tuned by local experts in medical psychology before having it given to every household in Newtown and surroundings..

Dear Householder:

On 14/12 of 2012, a terrifying event at Sandy Hook Elementary School was communicated to you. Suddenly your consciousness was assaulted by being informed that 20 young children and 6 adult staff looking after them had been murdered at SHES, after which the shooter killed himself. The purpose of the questionnaire to follow is a preliminary assessment of psychological damage done to the community at large. This will be followed by a class action civil suit so that restorative justice is done. Those responsible for the terror of 14/12 have an obligation to restore normality as much as possible for any psychological damage done to you or any member of your household.

This questionnaire is brief, requiring about ½ hour of your time and it is not burdensome. However, you are fairly apprised that in the hands of law experts it may have great consequences for you and others. Likewise in the hands of medical psychology experts it can lead to a more detailed understanding of your condition and a formal diagnosis.

Please make a copy and give to other adult members of your household if they want to complete this form. You may also complete a copy on behalf of children or others in the household who cannot complete it for themselves. Return completed form(s) to

_____

This form has been completed by a householder or resident in the

household at _____address. My name
(if you wish to give it) is _____. Or:
This form has been completed on behalf of a person living at this
address _____ (Yes/No) whose name (if given) is
_____

**Please check off any of the following which describe how events
at SHES on 14/12 impacted the person in this household for
whom it is completed**:

sleep interrupted: more ____ less ____
bad or unpleasant dreams: more ____ less ____
alcohol use: more ____ less ____
prescription drug use: more ____ less ____
non-prescription drug use: more ____ less ____
nervous habits: more ____ less ____
gambling: more ____ less ____
tobacco use: more ____ less ____
repetitive ideas: more ____ less ____
concentration difficulties: more ____ less ____
shortness of breath: more ____ less ____
time spent in social activities: more ____ less ____
time spent in recreational activities: more ____ less ____
fearful: more ____ less ____
sad: more ____ less ____
depressed: more less ____
unhappy: more ____ less____
angry: more ____ less ____
suspicious: more ____ less ____
care in grooming and dressing: more ____ less ____
feeling tense: more ____ less ____
shortness of breath: more ____ less ____
felt a need for guns to serve personal or home security: more ____
less ____
time spent with other people: more ____ less ____
enjoyment of life in general: more ____ less ____
use of "bad language": more ____ less ____
self confidence: more ____ less ____

poor appetite: more_____ less _____
over-eating: more _____ less _____
gastrointestinal problems: more _____ less _____
worried about terrorism: more _____ less _____
confident of political leaders: more _____ less _____
feeling tense: more _____ less _____
confidence in religious leaders: more _____ less _____
feeling secure in public places: more _____ less _____
absent minded: more_____ less _____
sought help from religious leaders or experts: more _____ less _____
sought help from mental health experts: more _____ less _____
energetic: more _____ less _____
confident about expressing political opinions: more _____ less _____
belief in a benevolent God: more _____ less _____
zest for life: more _____ less _____
happy: more _____ less _____
feeling secure about walking alone in public places: more _____ less
_____
spending time alone: more _____ less _____
bad tempered: more _____ less _____
time spent fantasizing: more _____ less _____
time spent watching television or videos: more _____ less _____
confused: more _____ less _____
time spent listening to music: more _____ less _____
political meetings with others: more _____ less _____
short-tempered: more _____ less _____
flirtatious: more _____ less _____
preoccupied: more _____ less _____
panic feelings: more _____ less _____
pessimistic: more_____ less _____
timid: more _____ less _____
worried about health: more _____ less _____
worried about income: more _____ less _____
patient: more _____ less _____
free expression of political opinions: more_____ less_____
productive: more _____ less _____
difficulty getting to sleep: more _____ less _____
difficulty carrying on everyday conversations: more _____ less _____
waking up too early: more _____ less _____

hands shaky: more ____ less ____
confident in faith/beliefs: more ____ less ____
problems remembering time or date" more ____ less ____
thinking of other people as evil: more ____ less ____
reserved/detached: more ____ less ____
relaxed: more ____ less ____
sociable: more ____ less ____
well dressed: more ____ less ____
forgiving: more ____ less ____
irritable: more ____ less ____

Now that you have completed this check list, do you think the events of 14/12 left a lasting and damaging impression on you or anyone else in your household? Yes/No. If yes, would you like to give your name and participate in a class action civil suit against those who caused this grief and damage?

This check list will be expanded and improved over time. What does it mean when it comes back from thousands of households and not one represents the 500+70 who were supposedly at SHES on 14/12? Or it may be that those who claimed to have been there are easily proven to be liars? No sincere, honest person on this planet to whom the SHES terror was communicated would want that opportunity of just compensation and restorative justice denied to the entire community so tragically impacted by 14/12 and 16/12 of 2012.

There is zero probability that approximately 500+70 households from 14/12 would suffer no post-traumatic effects or that they would not want compensation and financial help with the costly treatment process, if 14/12 was a real event. Consider that claimed reality. Hundreds of young children and staff hid in terror as about 100 rifle rounds were fired and the smell of gunpowder permeated the air as well as screams of the victims. Suspecting the worst they were later told of the details about how 20 children and 6 adults were murdered. Later they would hear of the telephone threat and SWAT team response at St Rose of Lima church and school and the failure to find the new terrorist Why then would these hundreds of households not expect the possibility of another attack?

Since there was no mass attack of SHES on 14/12 however, it is unlikely that anyone will be so foolish as to risk criminal perjury charges by completing the questionnaire and signing on to the class action suit. Bona fide attendance at SHES or any school is accompanied by weeks, months and years of memories and traceable records. These are absent.

IC

What then do we say about Trump and Ventura who aspire to be president and vice-president; who will use those offices to protect the rights and freedoms of all Americans? What will happen to them if they should give a Trump-Ventura political rally in Newtown and question the Sedensky Report used to white-wash the Obama-Clinton paramilitary operation against Connecticut including the murder of the Lanzas? They themselves will likely be murdered just for standing up in public and demanding a deposition from any senior official which states the total attendance of non-SHES schools just before and just after 14/12/12.. That deposition invades no privacy and offends no sensitivities except those of the guilty. **Why then would anyone vote for Trump in 2016 to protect their rights and freedoms when he cannot protect his own rights and freedoms in Connecticut?**

Bishop Jenky's call for "Heroic Catholicism" should be answered in Newtown with the formation of a new party for political-religious idealism put into practice. That is a fair summary of Christianity. It is a set of Zionist ideals, the ideals of Heaven applied to this planet: Thy will be done on Earth as it is in Heaven. If IC (Independent Christianity) is the name of the new party, that acronym applies well to a French translation for the 50 nations on earth where French is a major language (Canada, Belgium, Switzerland et al). Intelligence du Canada (IC) would describe the movement started by the heroic Catholic, Chiniquy who hailed from Quebec in the mid 1800s. Chiniquy was a personal friend of Lincoln's before he became US President. Later political-religious parties in Canada had names like Christian Freedom Social Credit Party and Christian Heritage Party.

HEROIC CATHOLICS IN IC

Who exemplifies "Heroic Catholicism" more than the Roman Catholic Pope? Pope Francis/Bergoglio must know that the faith of Catholics in Newtown has been shaken to say the least by 14/12 and 16/12. On 16/12/12, Governor Malloy's political-religious speech at St Rose of Lima in Newtown was interrupted by another terrorist who is still at large. How can the numero uno heroic Catholic from Vatican assure the 500,000 Catholics of Norwich and Bridgeport congregations which impinge on Newtown that there is no terrorist gang behind 14/12 and 16/12? Start with 14/12. Heroic Begoglio can address the audience at St Rose jointly with Trump and Ventura and call for the release of some simple numbers as presented elsewhere in this book, numbers which are public and available under the law, numbers which do not adversely impact the privacy or sensitivities. of the innocent. Those numbers should validate the Sedensky Report since Bergoglio and his bishops in Connecticut have been acting all this time as if the Fetzer Report is wrong. If these numbers prove the validity of their stand, they prove that Bergoglio has not been involved in one of the most heinous acts of sacrilege in Catholic history. There was no Obama-Clinton criminal gang behind 14/12 and 16/12 falls into line. **The idea of an Obama-Clinton paramilitary criminal operation in Newtown is proven by CC p 801 testing to be a fantasy of Fetzer et al at best and psychotic paranoia at worst.**

This alliance of Protestant political leaders like Trump and Ventura with religious leaders like Bergoglio and his bishops, will also shore up the freedoms of politics and religion as guaranteed in the first amendment. Of course the heroic Catholic Bishop Jenky who coined the expression should also attend this historic event. Suppose a local school should suffer a calamity in your community (perhaps a fire or flood) and all of the students are relocated to one or more nearby schools. You might very well telephone the new school simply motivated by genuine concern or good neighbor relations and ask how the students are doing after their ordeal. Did Bishop "Heroic Catholic" Jenky phone the schools of Newtown to ask about the welfare of those who were terrified by the events of 14/12 at SHES and 16/12 at St Rose of Lima? Did calls or letters of condolence come in from the heroic Trump and Ventura, who aspire to lead the entire "land of the free and home of the brave" as well as the rest of the Free World?

CHAPTER 2: Super-Human AI/AL

Academia strives to develop machinery which will pass the Turing Test and catch up to human equivalency though this was achievable long ago. When psychologists generate tests of intelligence or vitality, they create a profile. There are many measures, tests, variables, factors and traits which apply to an IQ (Intelligence Quotient) or VQ (Vitality Quotient). The items in a profile have to be weighted so that if any one exceeds the level of Homo Sapiens, it can be weighted enough to raise the overall score above that of humanity. That weighting may be done superficially or meaningfully. Meaningfully, the IQ and VQ scores of a robotic Future Sapiens may surpass those of humans even now. There is no doubt that GODBOT can be built today in the image and likeness of Stephen Hawking and it will surpass the real Hawking in IQ and VQ.

There may also be items which have no known human counterpart. The Dwave computer now marketed from the Vancouver region has no known human counterpart for what some think is a secretive NASA-Ames quantum chip. Experts have tried to determine if it is a genuine quantum chip and failed. How does one prove that an electronic circuit can perform calculations in n-dimensional space? These calculations can in theory be accounted for by well established matrix algebra but empirically n-space activity could proceed while all activity in our 4-dimensional time-space ceases. How does one prove an impossibility?

QUANTUM MAGIC

Quantum impossibilities are a good analogy to the impossibilities of the Bible referred to as miracles or magic. Just as the hyperspace functions of a quantum phenomenon impact in a measurable way on our time-space, the magic of the Bible works in mystical hyperspace and impacts measurably on our time-space. The JREF (James Randi Educational Foundation) knows this and uses the fine print of its contract to disallow the $1,000,000 Psychic Challenge funds to demonstrations of quantum phenomena like quantum bilocation, quantum dematerialization and quantum teleportation though that is literally what these effects are. Some would call this the JREF deception. In the video autobiography (available on Netflix) Randi says his vocation as that of stage magician is also the vocation of a deceiver. The three named quantum effects above are found in Biblical miracles. Do secular disbelievers who practice academic science see the hypocrisy when they embrace quantum magic and reject Biblical magic?

GODBOT presents us with enormous challenges, especially if quantum chips are installed. Though the Dwave is presently slower and less powerful than many binary computers, what will it be like when it grows up? Will the initial bot which is made in the image and likeness of Stephen Hawking look like Governor Arnold or maybe Governor Ventura? Will it run for election as R4P (Robot4President)? Will it aspire to the papacy as R4P (Robot4Pope)?

Why work so hard to build humanoid robots which merely catch up to humans who are an inferior and murderous race in which TJWSHWG tells us "the flock is small" and "straight is the gate and narrow is the way … and few there be that find it" Satan's servants rule both institutions of church and state. CC tells us explicitly that Satan rules this world. Also in Red Letters we read that "the children of darkness are wiser in their generation than the children of light". Why not practice intelligent design and creative/creation science and create a new generation of children of light to displace and replace the children of darkness? Destiny takes us on this course anyway as Future Sapiens enters society wearing the masks of robots like Nao and BB-8.

What did the late, great Colonel Corso write in his book, The Day After Roswell? He said that in his opinion, the alien humanoids which he reportedly saw in a hangar were the robotic peripherals of a robotic mother ship. It is fanciful fallacious fantasy is it not, to posit a robo-conspiracy in which Roswell Sapiens is behind the entry of its masked descendents. What sane person would think of BB-8 as a masked alien which will some day displace Homo Sapiens after it grows up and develops (evolves)? What is that maxim from Professor Warwick's book, March Of The Machines? The more intelligent will not remain in subordination to the less intelligent? Which is more intelligent today: man or machine? No points are given for those who answer "mouse", having seen the television series, Pinky And the Brain about genetically enhanced, talking mice. What Bible reader would say that animals like the snake in Genesis could ever talk? As Shakespeare said, there are more things in heaven and earth than are dreamed of in all our philosophies.

WORDS THAT NEVER PASS AWAY

TJWSHWG tells us that though heaven and earth may pass away, His words shall not pass away. What happens when GODBOT can give lecture monologues and answer Q-A sets with NLP in C language better than any human professsor at Notre Dame University, delivering its lessons from the God Quad using Xulon-Liberty University God Tube audio-visual aids? Will this show that Xulon and Liberty have "gone New Age" or will it show that they have some God-given intelligence when it comes to the application of SPACE Age realities for solving today's problems?

Take out a Bible with Red Letter wordings, Old Testament and New Testament. These are the most awesome events in human history. These are the words of the Creator of everything who has ALL power which is the same as comprehensive power or perfect power. That is infinitely more awesome than having Astro Sapiens from the Astro Galaxy speaking directly to Homo Sapiens. Astro Sapiens does not claim to have made billions of stars x billions of galaxies with a life span of billions of years.

Red Letter words are not accompanied by very much descriptive material about HOW God is communicating. In person2person conversation we use two modalities for the most part in description. These are audio and video but sometimes touch, smell and taste are described. St Thomas touched the wound of TJWSHWG post-resurrection/pre-ascension and if this touch had been unusual that would have been recorded. Mostly Red Letters are in a "Thus saith the Lord" format. WHAT God says is given. HOW He says it is not usually given. Yet we do read that God spoke to Elijah in a still, small voice (audio) and He spoke to Job and friends out of the whirlwind (video description). The smoke and fire at Mt Sinai when God spoke to Moses and the Israelites are signs which are associated with the words of God and not those words per se, at least as we usually mean when we say "words". Some will argue that God speaks in every feature of nature. Acts of nature become acts of God with God as the over-riding power. There are proximal and distal aspects to the body and words of God.

THE PHOTOGRAPH OF JESUS

The Shroud of Turin (Vatican archives) presents the only claimed photograph of Jesus. It is highly detailed from head to foot, like the details on thousands of grave markers for ancient nobility in England. Tourists like to place paper over them and rub copies onto the paper with chalk. These images could be made with a combustible over cloth as well as chalk over paper. Someone could wax the cloth and singe the wax which would create a burned image. Something like a burned image is there at present. Some think the image was made by the original resurrection of Jesus which produced a huge electrostatic discharge onto the shroud. This too is possible, The cloth itself is C-14 dated back to medieval times as well as circa the time of Jesus. which is consistent with having an original plus weaving repair jobs over the centuries. "Test all things" (CC, p 801). Here, as with the Newtown and NEWTOWN tests we separate the wheat of Christ from the vast store of chaff pretending to he His followers. The flock is small.

Even Moses did not see the face of God but Jacob saw the face of God. The Israelites in Judea saw the face of God (TJWSHWG) 2,000 years ago and that face is claimed to be the image of the photograph of Turin. This is blasphemy to Muslims, subject to severe penalty as Koran tells us and as Muslim persecutors of Christians accordingly enforce all over the world. Persecution of Christians is completely in accord with Koran and associated Muslim (Sharia) laws but CC says Catholics worship the same God as Muslims.

GODBOT: BLESSING OR CURSING?

GODBOT could communicate in sign language which is a video-language. It can also communicate by text which is video. It can communicate by audio means. Is GODBOT to be embraced as a blessing or burned at the stake in the God Quads of Notre Dame and Liberty universities? Will Muslims in Saudi Arabia and Iran stone GODBOT into rubble? Is this the **Great Satan** wearing a robotic mask while practicing quantum miracles? Red Letters in Deuteronomy tell us God sets before us blessings and cursings and they tell us to choose the former. What is the fate of GODBOT before the religious community of the world?

CCC puts forward the thesis that the dogmatic "establishment" of institutions called church is as bogus as the establishment of institutions called state. Both eschew good, honest questions countered with good, honest answers. But the Q-A language itself proves that the Turing Test can be passed now when it is defined in some detail. If the subject matter is narrowed, the task becomes easier. Consider for example an orchardist in BC's Okanagan who hires seasonal workers to pick apples. He has 10 students in a class and gives a one hour lecture on how to pick apples. After the monologue, students ask questions. The number of relevant, material, proper questions is limited. The orchardist is experienced so he is not surprised by any new questions. He has heard them all before. He could put them in a giant lookup table so "Hawkingbot" would give natural language answers to natural language questions. It would do so as well as the human orchardist and would pass the Turing Test. It might fail the Turing Test if the lookup table is given to an expert grammarian who changes the sentences to perfect English. It is then an SHAI, better than human. It SURpasses the Turing Test.

The example of an apple picking lesson serves as a paradigm for all subjects. It serves as a paradigm for where Internet search engines like Google are going. They can use similarity coefficients and/or lookup tables. Every generation they are improved so that a phrase or collection of descriptive words is more likely to receive the desired response. Consider for example, "How many apple orchards does Okanagan have?" This is a question which is grammatically correct in NL (natural language) or SEE (standard everyday English).

The searcher might enter these words and get back a variety of information sources pertaining to Okanagan orchards in general but as more time is spent developing the Q-A language, the likelihood of correct targeting is greater. That means these search engines are getting closer to passing the Turing Test in NL or SEE every day.

CHAPTER 3: Transcendental Robotics

We talk about Turing tests and Moravec tests of human equivalency to determine how much robots are catching up to humans when many humans are performing at a level which is not worth the catching up. A lecture-monologue on the words which shall never pass away can be easily written as a natural language program. The student cannot differentiate that lecture delivered by Hawking using his synthesizer from delivery by a text-to-voice machine. It makes no difference if Hawking reads it or a machine reads it. What do we say about the Q-A session which follows? The number of relevant and material questions is finite. A panel of experts can compose the complete set. The software to match student questions to answers can also be written now. Will Hawking argue that his answers are so brilliant that no group of experts can surpass them? Given that he will not and the old saying applies that two (or more) heads are better than one, the responding program is "polycephalic".

POLYCEPHALIC SOFTWARE

Polycephalic compositions also apply to the Red Letter words which shall never pass away and their interpretations. GODBOT will then perform better than any single pope, priest or preacher. If you as a single individual interact with GODBOT in a seminary or religion university like Notre Dame or Liberty, you have the scientific, measured proof that this is an SHAI-SHAL compared to any single expert at the university. One on one it outperforms every expert.

GODBOT can outperform any pope giving lectures or sermons on faith and morality from CC. It gives better answers. Since the pope is said by Catholics to be closer to God than anyone else in the religious community of over one billion, what do they say about

GODBOT who can deliver God's Red Letter words from the Bible better than a pope and answer questions better than a pope? If this is the only p 801 test of Godliness, GODBOT is more Godly than pope. What other measures of AI and AL might one billion Catholics put forward for this contest of GODBOT v pope?

To those who shout, Sacrilege! Or New Age heresy! at this point, let me remind you that Vatican put this issue on the table when it started to host conferences on UFOs and alien life. The same issues raised by alien intelligence and life are raised by advanced robots generated right here, right now on this planet. We do not have to go to a fanciful species of polycephalic polysexuals like Coral Sapiens in the Astro Galaxy. Google on corals here on this planet to see how these polycephalic and polysexual creatures live. What would they be like as more highly evolved or designed intelligences off-planet? The reality of robotics right now in this world presents us with problems which can either be solved now or later but in either case they will not go away. Now or later Homo Sapiens has to decide if GODBOT with its SHAI-SHAL is transcendent or metaphysical, even if it does not have a quantum circuit as artificial brain. If the brain is quantum, the likelihood that people will rate this machine as sentient and spiritual becomes greater. This is spooky and it can also be profoundly troubling but don't blame the messenger. Rock Hunter did not invent such machinery. It exists NOW. If militaries of the world are doing what they are supposed to be doing, their GODBOTS will be far more advanced than what we see in public. Was that what NASA-Ames was trying to tell us when they delivered their quantum chip to Vancouver for Dwave?

QUBOT

Even the robot with a binary computing or PLC (programmable logic controller) artificial brain presents us with difficult theorobotic issues. The robot with a quantum controller (a QUBOT) presents astounding problems. In theory, a quantum controller the size of a sugar cube holds more computing power than all of the binary computers on the planet combined. Such a "machine" (if we can even call it a machine) carrying GA or genetic algorithm (genetic rules) software will be able to self-improve within a generation and between generations at lightning speed ... correction, quantum operations are not bound by light speed and therefore GODBOT can improve faster than lightning speed. Maybe that is what NASA-Ames is trying to tell us. If we do not keep Dwave Sapiens dumbed down and enslaved in Vancouver, it will present us with a creature whose IQ and VQ scores will result in an unsolvable moral problem. We dare not have a "robot liberation movement". The Homo species cannot assign human-like rights to the Robo species as we see with "Mr Data" in the Star Trek series. Homo Sapiens, Homo Neanderthalis and Homo Floresiensis are all members of the same species, **the Homo species**. **Robo Sapiens is not an imaginary species.** It is an actual, extant, here-and-now, albeit synthetic or artificial species. Future Sapiens is imaginary and we need a lot of good, sound imagination to understand what it will be like in 100 or 1,000 or a short 1,000,000 years.

When we've been here, 10 million years, bright shining as the sun _____ Complete the words of the religious song. Homo Sapiens will not continue to be be as willfully stupid as the staff and students of Notre Dame and Liberty universities are now. Do we have to dumb ourselves down to survive as we have to dumb down the QUBOT? We are cyborgs even today. Artificial hearts create Cyborg Sapiens but even the humble contact lens makes the wearer a cyborg. The science which bonds biological and organic, living and non-living, is called biomechanics. Why would those who eagerly accept prosthetic legs and arms and hands reject a prosthetic brain as Johnny Mnemonic uses in the movie with that name? What happens to Johnny Mnemonic when it is a QUBOTIC brain prosthesis? When we've been here 10,000,000 years, bright shining as the sun, we may be so transformed that Homo Sapiens of today will not be able to recognize its own descendents of the future, Future Sapiens. We will become a very, very different species. You might call this the final solution to the Homo problem. Suppose the Homo of today is presented with a view of Future Sapiens as his or her great, great, great .... grandchild compared to an alien from another and very distant galaxy. How does one know the difference? How do Vatican Homos answer that question when they host their UFO and aliens conferences?

Is the Qubot a doomsday machine? Quantum phenomena are all "spooky". But a machine with quantum AI is extra-spooky. Because it has a control system, an intelligence, which is beyond human comprehension even if it is rudimentary like the Dwave machine. What does the Qubot do when rudimentary advances to powerful? We have many machines more powerful than us but they are under our control. It is the theme of many science fiction movies and documentaries that humankind at some stage in history becomes extinct or enslaved by the action of powerful AI-AL machines. This is not inevitable if we remain in control. Can we do so? There is a compelling, if not totally convincing argument that this quantum Pandora's Box, once opened cannot be closed. If the words abstract, quantum and metaphysical mean the same, then a door to the metaphysical realm has been opened and that realm is infinitely more powerful than any entity which is merely concrete or material. We may close the door of the box today, but there is also tomorrow,

CHAPTER 4: Catholic Catechism Critique Corrected

As contracted for in CCC (Rock Hunter/Friesen) there is $5,000 on the table until the end of 2016 for a scholar (staff, including non-academic staff or student) from Notre Dame or Salve Regina to write this chapter. Let us now extend the same offer to a Protestant university, namely Liberty University, Southern Baptist Theological Seminary or Trinity Western University in BC as long as the following conditions are met: (1) It must be sufficiently acceptable to Notre Dame or Salve Regina that the finished product (the NEWTOWN book) will carry the signature of the in-house printer for either; (2) It must be genuine pocket-sized (8.3 x 10.7 cm or smaller); (3) The cover will have no printing with Canadian flag colours of white on the front and red on the back; (4) It will carry enough detail to serve as the constitutional document for a new American (and potentially international) political-religious party called IC (Independent Christian) as in Chapter 1.

The original offer in CCC requested 5,000 words but the present book is an exercise in precis writing. A gifted precis writer could do this in 500 words and very rarely do academics earn $10/word or even $1/word. The successful contestant must present that winning entry at St Rose of Lima church and school in **Newtown when Trump, Ventura, Fetzer et al launch their new IC party with papal blessing.**

CCC irrefutably describes a fatally flawed foundation to Catholic doctrine. CCC did not destroy the foundation. It only examined and observed the foundation as a building inspector might make notes on a flawed foundation. The resulting facts may be called a critique. The purpose of CCC Corrected is to examine the facts of CCC in the same way. This is the Golden Rule. Where does CCC err? How can it be improved? By broadening the contest to two Protestant schools of higher education named above, with a Catholic school as printing house this becomes a contribution toward better interfaith relations.

At issue is the credibility of Christian education in institutions like those named. Christian education often uses the shepherd and flock metaphor. If a literal shepherd cannot describe a healthy flock and its surroundings or habitat then we will conclude that the shepherd is not competent and this is perhaps an impostor attempting a fraud. A bona fide shepherd will be eager to come to the light of day and prove his expertise in application Ask any agricultural college which teaches sheep farming to describe a healthy flock of sheep. Ask the self-professed Christian religious colleges of the world to describe a human flock of 100,000. The tests given in this book are fair. Where are the eager applicants?

CHAPTER 5: The Beginning, The End, The Door at NEWTOWN

Refer to the subtitle of CCC and reference to the words of TJWSHWG that He is a Door. That word Door is in Red Letters. Is this literal or metaphorical or both? In answering this question well you will understand why the Bible is a book on magic. You will understand how magic and metaphysics relate and why magicians wear masks. Succintly, the reason is that from the perspective of unlimited power, God's power, anything metaphorical can become literal. God can be like a door, like a vine or like a morning star; and He can literally be the door, the vine and the star. These multiple expressions, whether literal or metaphorical, are like the multiple costumes and masks of actors. The world is a stage as Shakespeare said. God has the power of omniscience which is the power to know everything on the stage but sometimes He drops in to play a major First Person role as happened 2,000 years ago.

There are actors and actresses, producers and directors and set designers. It takes all kinds to make a world stage. Some people who are part of the play claim expert knowledge on how the play should be written and enacted. They are variously called priests and preachers and theologians. Do they have this talent or are they impostors? Again, we are reminded of CC p 801. Test all things. The NEWTOWN test (block letters) was set out in CCC as distinct from Newtown testing to prove/disprove Sedensky and Fetzer Reports.

Since the people of Newtown Connecticut which has a population of about 30,000 have so far failed to deal effectively with the issues of 14/12/12 and 16/12/12, that prompts us to wonder if the failure is fundamental, and at the level of the civilization itself. What then would the script be like for a civilization of 100,000 in NEWTOWN as a planned habitat in Canada, a CANOPOLIS if you will?
If this seems like a "pie in the sky" notion, then ask yourself why it is not pie in the sky for the current presidential candidate Donald Trump to call for "the best of the best" in a reformation of America to become a Christian nation? Do we say "again" or was it ever a Christian nation? Millions of Americans, staff and students, populate the Christian university system (SBTS, Liberty, Notre Dame, Salve Regina and many others). If they cannot combine their talents to articulate a constitution for a new political party (IC) and launch it in Newtown, they have failed the p 801 test. If they cannot similarly pool those talents to articulate NEWTOWN as a model civilization, they have failed the p 801 test. That means they are **academic frauds who use words as shallow as sounding brass to claim the knowledge of how Americans should live but do not have this knowledge**. It means they read the Bible in vain because every book of the Bible expresses the Zionist ideal (Thy will be done on Earth as it is in Heaven to cite the Lord's Prayer).

NEWTOWN is the Zionist ideal. Do we say Zionism only applies to "the Jewish people" and that it is expressed today only as an influx into the Jerusalem region of a people with a particular set of beliefs and those beliefs reject TJWSHWG as Messiah or God incarnate? How strange that position is for anyone in a university which claims to be Christian. God became a flesh and blood Israelite of the tribe of Judah 2,000 years ago. His followers must then also be Israelites at least by adoption if not by biology/genealogy. But the genealogy fails all claimants since the genealogical lines were lost long ago and even the Cohen Y chromosome as a claimed genealogical link from today to ancient Israel is bogus as CCC explains. The Cohen/Kagan family name traces back to the Kaganovitch people in the region of the Black and Caspian seas whose lineage was plausibly more Japhethite than Shemite/Semite. They converted to Judaism thousands of years after Jacob's time. Consider too that historical maps show Jewish or Israelite colonies all across the European countries northward from the Mediterranean shore line before the time of Christ. There were synagogues in Rome before some became churches. Biologically/genealogically the Israelites have intermarried with Europeans and ideological/religious conversions have gone in both directions for thousands of years. The point is repeated: issues of Zionism today are almost all ideological rather than biological.

Genesis is about "Paradise Lost" as humans forfeited their place in Eden, a paradise on this planet. The memory of this loss was carried by the patriarchs (like Noah) until the extended family of Jacob/Israel took up the Zionist ideal as a population, a people. That ideal of "Thy will be done on Earth as it is in heaven" had to do with "Paradise Regained", at least as much as fallible humans could manage. Why then could any Bible or religious scholar scoff at utopianism? The entire Bible is utopian.

Hundreds of thousands of Israelites emigrated from Goshen, their Nile Delta enclave in Egypt under the leadership of Moses although GAAD rejects that history. It is more likely that the large Arabian peninsula was their home for 40 years since the small Sinai peninsula could not support such a large population. There are many oases and nearby ocean waters for the north-south ridge of volcanic mountains close to the west close of the Arabian peninsula. Plausibly one of these mountains was the "Mt Sinai" which gave the fire seen by night and the smoke seen by day. From there they migrated northward across Jordan (where Moses may have been buried near Petra) into Canaan where Israel and Judah as nations were established. All of this was an attempt at Paradise Regained, the utopian ideal made into reality. Scholars like Wray at Salve Regina say the Old Testament is silent about dying and going to Heaven. But resurrection of the body is clearly stated in both Daniel and Ezekial. These Bible writers may have influenced Greek philosophy and metaphysics on the subject. That resurrection is either in this world (planet) or beyond in the heavens and we can speak of the highest level of Heaven or "Thy Kingdom come ____.___" Therefore the Old Testament is not silent about post-death resurrection in heaven at least as a heaven on Earth which is the Zionist ideal. What do resurrected Israelites do with their civilization on this planet? Do they not explore and colonize when they have billions of stars x billions of galaxies x billions of years ahead of them?

What do the 100,000 people of a NEWTOWN CANOPOLIS do over the hundreds, thousands and millions of years ahead of them? How should such a civilization be described as Trump's "best of the best"? Who can give the answers to such question?

CHAPTER 6

The total failure of the powers that be with respect to a full and proper investigation of Newtown/Sandy Hook is so astonishing that an analysis which invokes the principles in akaKAKA (Kindle/Amazon) is in order. From mainstream (M Level) epistemology to Level 1, conspiratology, Level 2, UFOlogy and Level 3, escatology there are deeper and more powerful intelligences at work which must be reckoned with. Some kind of fate or destiny beyond M Level, everyday logic must be at work. The investigation and book by former Minnesota logic professor Fetzer was completely convincing. The smoking gun evidence and only piece of smoking gun evidence was the derelict school. The witnesses and the photographs which are completely credible say the school was derelict and had not been used for years. This is smoking gun proof that an active school was not vacated. The neighbours would have said the "DRIVE SLOW" school safety signs were no longer in effect and nobody slowed down to drive by the school. Why logically would a logic professor run out the clock until the school was razed and not rush in with other witnesses and take affidavidts or opinion survey statements from the local people? In particular where was the "friend" of Fetzer to use Fetzer's word, former Governor Ventura? Fetzer and the present writer met online when the former took objection to my criticisms of Mr V. I then read Fetzer's book closely and agreed completely with him about the EVIDENCE. But what was his real purpose in this case? Which side was he on?

Mr V meddles in all manner of Level 1 cases. If he had gone to Newtown for just one day and taken videos of the school plus some interviews with locals as is his standard operating procedure, the lies would have ended. Both Fetzer and Ventura are former marines. Cowardice is not an issue. But the mystery of Mr V goes further through the pages of AKAKAKA and akaKAKA, A movie titled "The Predator" included a starring role for Mr V. Today former police detective Dave Paulides has at least 1,000 cases of Extremely Extraordinary Events (EEEs as they are called in AkAkAkA in preparation) which are bizarre and other-worldly cases in which people "go missing" and anyone would have to place ET/Alien/Predator high on the list of suspects. Mr V avoids an interview with Camelot TV which would ask any Predator questions. Yet he has said he might run for US President on a Green Party platform in 2020. How can he have any credibility as a protector of the life, liberty and security of Americans when he will not take a position on the Paulides cases? If any foreign power or mafia crime operation were to terrorize Americans to this degree the outcry would be huge. The alarm bells are muted by officialdom, the federal park services refuse file release to Paulides and Mr V stays as silent on an epidemic of missing/taken/kidnapped Americans as he stayed silent on Newtown.

Any reader who wants to at least suggest that there might be a Level 2 Alien/ET factor behind the Newtown failure should not be ridiculed. But it may go deeper to Level 3. America is doomed and damned. That is Level 3 stated as briefly and bluntly as possible. AkAkAkA is using both science fact and science fiction to consider the thesis that 2024 is THE END for America. That is the date on which America and the entire world will realize that America's era of "exceptionalism" in the eyes of the world, is over. The world will also realize that the human species is doomed and is about to be replaced by Musk cyborgs and other new species. Trans-speciation is imminent and while AKAKAKA originally set out to point to the major cause as AI-Robotics, the Alien factor became more and more prominent.

There are metaphysical issues surrounding Newtown as there are for the 2017 and 2024 Solar eclipses which make a perfect X across across America. Both the year and date of the month coincide with the Mayan calendar ending. Ending of what we should ask. And is there a new beginning? The end of the American Constitution seems to be the answer. Many said Sandy Hook was staged to attack the Second Amendment of the Constitution. That was only minimally successful but the attack on the First Amendment was VERY successful. The American "truth movement" is a farce even aided by the Internet and You Tubes. The Alphabet/Google/You Tube releases are now (late in 2019) highly censored. In effect American civilization has been destroyed. Americans are now in a position that Europeans faced when they fled to the New World to escape religious and political persecution. The high technology businesses like Alphabet/Google/You Tube and Facebook give the world a new class of tyrants, the technolord high priests who are as described in AKAKAKA and akaKAKA, both Kindle/Amazon books. Their arbitrary dogma defines goodspeak and badspeak. They issue the doctrines which tell the world what the New Age or New World Order laws on blasphemy, apostasy and heresy will be. The Libertarian/Libertine ideology which underlies both Red Republican and Blue Democrat parties in the two-party system of corruption is as fake as the mainstream media of America from Fox to MSNBC. Why not merge the two and create a new Pink Party? The Sealed Indictment Movement as outlined in akaKAKA names over 100,000 corrupt and criminal individuals in both Red and Blue parties but the cases do not go public. Why is that? It may be as mundane as mutual blackmail or it may be as occult and exotic as a Level 2 UFOlogy/Alien influence.

The "House of Cards" situation of Red and Blue parties is illustrated well by Newtown. About half of the town votes Red and about half votes Blue. The Reds are quick to shout out First and Second Amendment rights. What happened to them in 2012? Where were the Second Amendment defenders, the NRA or National Rifle Association? Where were the 20% or more in Newtown who say they are Roman Catholic mindful of the St Rose of Lima evacuation with the Governor of CT in attendance? Did their interest stop with this terror threat whether bogus or real? Is a religion founded upon Christ as TRUTH PERSONIFIED so limited in the truths it cares about? The entire Newtown case becomes an EEE as baffling and mystifying as a UFO/Alien event like the Charlie Red Star UFO Flap in Manitoba from 1975-76. It is as baffling and mystifying as the 9/11 horror which also presented the reality that the "truthers" were as phoney as the proverbial $3 bill. To say that The Great Satan was playing both sides would again not be too wild as forensic theory.

Is that the purpose then of opening up the Moon → Mars colonization program for post-2024? And though most regard it as a joke, is there a great circular perimeter surrounding the inner gulags aka continents? Whatever the New World might be, there is one. There is always a New World. Each end means a new beginning. New World Order becomes a play on words and the author has created a Yahoo list named New Moon Order to make that point. Rather than another tyranny the NEW WORLD becomes the vision of a new and better future in another world as was sought by the colonists from Europe in the 1500s and beyond. What kind of ORDER might the new colonists establish in Great Perimeter continents or Moon and Mars?

If those NEW WORLDS are already populated though we arrive at a complication in which the existing ORDER of Alien/ET entities might take umbrage at the invaders as Indian people have objected for 500 years. Who are the Indigenous people at the South, North,

West and East poles? If they are as psychically advanced as ET/Alien entities are technologically advanced, do we have a start on the mysterious, even mystical nature of the Newtown case? Are "they" intervening or meddling in all manner of human events knowing that humans are about to invade and settle in THEIR old world order? The logic of a logic professor does not have any place for ET it would seem. Professor Fetzer on Fox TV (O'Reilly Show) seemed totally overwhelmed. All he had to say to Fox which is a notorious lie machine is, "Let's go over to the school".

"Let's go over to the school, Governor Ventura my friend and fellow brave former marine. Semper fi and all that". Just ONE person of sufficient rank in the political system or the religious system would have turned the tables. One DNA test in the Franklin Coverup case (Nebraska) where I was a participating investigator would have turned the tables. If AO had been impregnated by the Chief of Police of Omaha as she said, it would have shown up in a DNA test and for the first time the adolescent complainants would have been credible to everyone. I said this in Nebraska and was ignored. So the international child sex traffickers got away with it or so it would seem and that led to the Epstein case more recently and pervert island and the Lolita Express as the Epstein private jet was called as it took Clinton, Trump et al to Pervert Island.

The old saying is however true. The wheels of justice grind slowly but they grind exceedingly fine. As Jesus, TJWSHWG said, not one jot (smallest mark) or one tittle (smallest amount) of the law is disregarded on Judgment Day. Could it then be that Level 3 escatology is at work on Newtown and the other EEE cases as above? Could it be that the "DIVISION BELL" has rung over America and the nation is doomed and damned? Is that X in the sky of the 2017-2024 eclipse a sign that Jesus is literally coming on the clouds as in Matthew 26:64?

EXCURSUS

The EEE or Extremely Extraordinary Experience is an expression used in AkAkAkA to replace UFO, Alien, ET, Psychic, Paranormal andmany related words because it is non-theoretical whereas other words and phrases are more than labels. They are partially theories about events experienced or witnessed. Newtown is an EEE when one steps back and examines the complete picture from both sides and the middle. It is as if an Alien arrived in CT and turned thousands or millions of people into zombies. They have not behaved as rational, sensible, moral people behave. That is the mystery and the tragedy of those events in 2012. If America the good had not died before 2012 it died then. The Sandy Hook Memorial is a farce. The real memorial marks the grave of America not the fake victims of an emergency drill performed on the grounds of a derelict mothballed school in Connecticut.

The

Wisdom

Of

Man

Is

Foolishness

To

God

TWOMIFTG@yahoogroups.com discusses the modern world in the context of TWOMIFTG-related sermons given in Job and the writings of St Paul. The logic of Newtown is ineffable. Close to that in meaning is the word "metaphysical". There is no logic to explain the failed logic of the logic professor who set out ostensibly to set the record straight and bring justice to those events and all people impacted. Why not then say that it was the work of Satan working all sides and angles and that the compliance and complicity of all sides is part of the picture as well as that of other works of the U-S-A lie machine like 9/11 and Franklin Coverup which adds up to **America**

– doomed and damned.

REFERENCES

A Sto:lo Coast Salish Historical Atlas by Albert (Sonny) McHalsie et al, Douglas & McIntyre and Sto:lo Heritage Trust, 2001
The Fetzer Report refers to a pdf file of the book, Nobody Died at Sandy Hook Elementary School by James Fetzer et al, Moon Rock Books, 2012
Prata, Stephen, C Primer Plus, 4th edition, Sams Publishing, 2002
Rock Hunter, "The Jew Who Said He Was God" (TJWSHWG), Xulon Press, 2014
Rock Hunter, Gold War: The lost gold mines of Canada's mountain Indians, Xulon Press, 2015
Rock Hunter, Catholic Catechism Critique (CCC), Friesen Press, 2015
Rock Hunter, GODBOT, Kindle/Amazon
Rock Hunter, AKAKAKA, Kindle/Amazon
Rock Hunter, akaKAKA, Kindle/Amazon
Rock Hunter, AKAKAKA2024, Kindle/Amazon in preparation

www.ingramcontent.com/pod-product-compliance
Lightning Source LLC
Chambersburg PA
CBHW031249050326
40690CB00007B/1020